Pensive Pearls

Voiceful Verses to Weigh

Jaya Karmalkar

Creative CROWS
PUBLISHERS LLP
the publishing & communication people

Published by

Office: A-42, Dayanand Colony,
New Delhi(South)-110024
Emails: ganivpanjrath@yahoo.co.in, tannaazirani@gmail.com

ISBN-13: 978-81-949782-2-0

ISBN 10: 81-949782-2-X

MRP: $25/-

Book size: 5.5*8.5

Printed and bound by Creative Crows Publishers LLP

Preface

The Pandemic which we all lived through has been unprecedented in more ways than one. It surely provided me with generous time for contemplation and introspection. As I started penning down my thoughts, one poem led to another and lo and behold! This compilation came into being. The whole process of composing poems has been cathartic. It surprised, comforted, uplifted, healed me and blessed me with wisdom. My poems depict a gamut of personal feelings ranging from wonder to unrest to reconciliation to realization to resolve, which I'm sure the readers can identify with and relate to. I hope it strikes a chord with them, which encourages me, to continue writing. I'd like to profusely thank Ganiv Panjrath and Tannaaz Irani of Creative Crows Publishers for their unstinting support and guidance.

Happy reading and do feel free to give me your suggestions and feedback.

Contents

A panoply of personal poems dealing with myriad inner feelings and introspective perspectives that the readers can identify and relate to.

About Love

*'**About Love**' very convincingly demonstrates the importance of giving love to receive the love that we desire. There's a gentleness in the poem which touches the heart.*

The language of love is universal

It's sweet as honey and gentle as a dove

and totally at our disposal

After all, to be loved, we all love

Just that...we have to first give

what we desire,

and carefully sieve

our behaviour, even if ourselves we overtire

and ultimately...our ties of love remain

and many inconsequential matters go down the drain

Love is the most beautiful emotion,

It works like a wondrous magic potion

Just that to be loving and forgiving isn't always easy

But it's worth trying... Do you agree?

If Only

'If Only' is a personal poem that very tenderly brings to the fore the regrets the poet has and ends on a positive note, wherein the poet wouldn't want to repeat the same mistakes and wouldn't want to be regretful in life. It's a thoughtful and touching poem.

If only...I could be more loving and kind

especially with those whom I'm not going to meet and find

If only...I could be more accommodating and giving

which has now becoming my way of living

If only...I could laugh and smile more

and prevent situations from getting sore

If only...more appreciative of life I could be

and more positivity, around me I could see

If only...I could be more grateful and thankful to God

and feel more comfortable than odd

Enough...,now I won't let these ifs pile

I'll follow my heart and feel good all the while

My Thoughts

*'**My Thoughts**' is an interesting poem that delightfully touches upon the impact of thoughts. The poem has a natural flow as well as a racy rhythm.*

My magnanimous mind allots

space to thoughts of various sorts

There are thoughts that ramble...

Some consciously amble

Some just scramble,

while some are prickly like bramble

Many thoughts into nothingness shamble,

but the best are the happy thoughts that glide and gambol

There are thoughts wherein I join the dots,

only to see through others' plans and plots,

There are thoughts that amuse and excite and delight,

not to forget thoughts they spur and incite

Then there are thoughts that take off on a flight

and thoughts which I want to hold on to, tight

There are thoughts which shock and thoughts which
pleasantly surprise

and in some, a lot of mystery lies...

Thoughts when not harnessed are like buzzing flies

but these days, my mind has become wise.

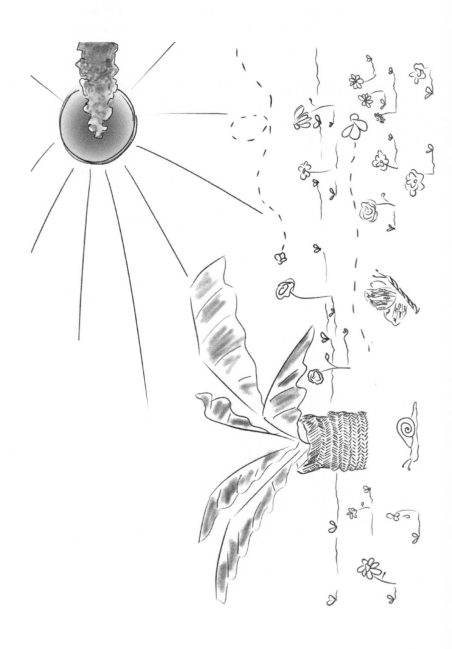

Each Morning

*'**Each Morning** 'is an inspiring poem, in which the poet projects the positive points of the morning in a racy and rhythmic manner.*

Each morning is like a new awakening

A new chapter, a new beginning,

Energizing, stimulating,

exciting and invigorating

Propelling us to get cracking

and send our inertia and lassitude packing

Each morning encourages us to take on the day

in the best possible way

as it ushers in a new ray of hope, a beacon of opportunity

to work towards achieving our goals in entirety

Each morning sends our morale spiraling on an upswing

Truly paeans about Mornings I'd love to sing

Colours In The Pandemic

'Colours In the Pandemic', deftly captures the interplay of colours and creates a bright canvas which is interwoven with rhythm and feelings which the reader can relate to. The poem is infused with vibrancy and has a sprightly tone.

Colours in my life have a very special place

Courtesy, the pandemic, which has made me gaze

at the redness of the rose with a smile on my face

and I can't help but praise

the several shades of green in my garden, so lovely,

right from the grass to the leaves of plants and trees...

I find the brown in the mud of my pots so very earthy

and surely the pinks of the bougainvillea, do please

my very being, as do the Golden sun-bathed patches

and when my glance catches

a colourful and beautiful butterfly,

my heart begins to sigh in sheer wonder

Ever since these colours I've begun

to admire and assimilate, me they stun

a little more, and flood me with happiness

Life is more colourful in the pandemic. Oh yes!

My Inner Strength

'My Inner Strength' is a pensive poem which talks about the various sources from which the poet draws her inner strength to carry on relentlessly.

My inner strength I draw,

from failures and constructive self-criticism

and positive auto-suggestion and realism...

At times...when dejection begins to claw

and my worries and anxieties begin to gnaw

with smarting wounds, excruciating and raw

and when all my mind does is hum and haw,

I turn inwards and examine each error and flaw

and let my agonies gradually thaw...

and climb my way to the other side of the seesaw

with positive steps and positive self-talk

which keep me steady as a rock

and act like protective layers

and certainly I derive my strength from fervent prayers

Evenings

*In The poem **'Evenings'** the poet very interestingly conveys her impression of evening as a special time of the day and the reasons why, evenings appeal to her. The images which the poet has employed are arresting and the poem is profound.*

Evenings bring with them a sense of calm

For me they hold a special charm...

As I sip my much desired coffee

and let a poised demeanour take over me

I run through the goings on of the day assuredly

Evenings bring with them walks, 'oh so leisurely '

and I like to see children playing away merrily

and fondly remember my childhood days so hassle free...

Sunsets bring an air of resignation and solemnity

and inspire me to be resilient and gritty

The dusk ushers in a sense of soberness so deep

and in my deportment as it begins to seep,

my heart jubilantly begins to leap,

as my admiration for evenings, I decide to keep

The Heart Knows

*'**The Heart Knows**' is a poem which dexterously portrays the importance of following one's heart and turning inwards for guidance and advice. The poem ends on a note of reassurance.*

When I'm down and out,

clouded with apprehension and self-doubt,

when my morale plunges into the depths of despair

and hope just doesn't seem to be there

when all I see is darkness and dismay

and my nerves begin to fray,

I turn to my heart and it lights up my way

and realise I surely do, that it's in the right place

as it comes up with remedies, clear as day...

and a smile flashes on my face

I profusely thank my heart as it definitely knows,

apart from celebrating highs, how to tackle, 'the lows'

Pandemic Moments

In 'Pandemic Moments' all kinds of memorable moments have been very beautifully described. The poem is simple yet sweet.

The Pandemic has helped me create

a mosaic, mind blowing and great,

of family moments, free flowing and funny,

sweet, salty and sunny

and magical, memorable and mushy.

These moments have enriched me tremendously;

I've consciously begun to take care of my mood

and check myself when my inner voice sounds rude

and as a result, a lot less I have erred

and how I love myself, when I put my best foot forward,

to watch tender moments emerge,

which in the centre of my heart, snugly converge

Prayers

*Prayers' deals with the positive effects it has on the poet, in an
absorbing style. The poem has a natural flow and has a gentle
tone*

Prayers have a power of their own

and this for a long time I have known

but in the pandemic prayers have acquired

a new meaning, and I 've got the peace I've desired

Like water quenches my thirst prayers satiate my soul

and they play an important role

In cleansing my heart and mind

when they get lined

with disturbances and dolour, dampening

A glimmer of hope prayers bring

They fill me with indebtedness and gratitude

and provide an insightful and enlightening interlude

I experience Zen like serenity and effortlessly I go

beyond myself and let my wishes flow

for the wellbeing of one and all

With prayers in my own eyes I stand tall

Pandemic Prudence

'Pandemic Prudence' *is evocative and reflective wherein the poet deals with problems   sensibly. It ends on a positive note.*

In search of solutions, I have swum in a sea

of worry and misery, only to be

as clueless as I had started out

and then I ask myself...why did I rout

my peace of mind and equanimity

and then wallow in self-pity?

As I delve deeper into my psyche

and connect with my inner being,

myself I begin to free

from self-inflicted torture and tumult and begin seeing

the importance of being collected and composed

no matter what; and since then, I have closed,

the door to negative overthinking, and found,

sure shot antidotes that appeal and also astound.

The Year 2020

*'**The Year 2020**' aptly describes the consequences of the pandemic and all that the poet has learnt from it. The readers can relate to it easily.*

Strange, Unpredictable and Offbeat

which made our travel plans retreat

These are the first thoughts which flood me,

when I talk of the year 2020...

A year when the pandemic took the world by storm

and staying indoors became the norm

A year when using masks, social distancing

and sanitizing hands would be the done thing

A year when online classes and working from home

began to intensify the desire to move out and roam

A year when we got to explore, scores

of activities and skills indoors.

A year that taught me not to take life for granted

and a year wherein, many values my mind planted

in my being...Well! The year just stood out,

for reasons, one can't doubt...

Pandemic Profundity

'Pandemic Profundity' is a poem that talks about a special connection the poet felt, with her surroundings and nature after the pandemic. The poet expresses her happiness on getting time to observe and appreciate the beauty of nature.

The Pandemic has made me value stepping outside

and breathing fresh air, more than ever before

and I've begun to take pride

in the flora and fauna aound and the greenery galore

which hitherto had missed my eye

Now I consciously try

to be mindful, of the birds winging their way, high in the sky,

I like the way I sigh

when I see blooming flowers, beautiful and bright

I'm also bowled over by the sight

of my kitchen garden, with baby vegetables so cute

and to the beauty of nature as I salute,

I thank the pandemic for making me view,

life's pleasures with admiration, so new.

About Friends

*'**About Friends**' throws light on the need to have good friends and most importantly on the need to be a friend in order to have good friends in one's life.*

It is said, 'We can't choose our family

but we can certainly choose our friends'

and rightly so, with friends, 'ourselves', we get to be

without any filters, veneers and amends

Friends are hope harbingers and surprise springers

They are all-time saviors and humdingers

Our problems they lighten

and our moods they uplift and brighten,

our joys and enthusiasm they heighten

and our resolve to achieve, they tighten

Our fears and insecurities they understand

and are ever ready to lend a helping hand

Their absence makes the ambience dull and bland

and their presence makes life ever so beautiful and grand

but...to have friends, one has to be one

Otherwise, we will be left with none.

My World

In 'My World' the poet has unfurled her world wherein she imagines scenes and situations that appeal to her and does interesting impersonation. It ends on a happy note.

My world within this world is, more than I can ask...

and in it I love to bask

It refreshes, consumes and cocoons me

In it, a lot of impressive impersonation I get to do

and different kinds of people I get to be...

and these vicarious thrills are too good to be true

In my world I conjure up scenes and situations

which I'm besotted with totally...

I enjoy the cordial interpersonal relations

that I have, with, so many...

I celebrate grandly, my victories which are entities

only in my world; and to enthrall they never cease...

In my world I love being my own boss

and letting my senses go for a toss...

In my world there's no room for pain and sorrow

and from life every now and then when I borrow,

some time to be in this utopian world of mine,

I'm more than happy, when my world and reality intertwine

Ever Since

*'**Ever Since**' is an upbeat and delightful poem which brings the positive consequences of the Pandemic. It's got a lively flow.*

Ever since the Pandemic hit us like storm,

my life has taken another form,

that's reflective, and encouraging me to be a homebody

and motivating me to read, write and study.

Staying consciously indoors for hours on end

has been a mixed blend

It has taught me to be adjustable and stoic

after I grew tired and sick

of the new routine, which had me toiling away,

day after day; and then one fine day,

to see the positive side I tried

and my acknowledgement I couldn't hide

I now take the Pandemic challenges in my stride

and my own inner strength leaves me wide eyed!

Pandemic Pleasures

*'**Pandemic Pleasures**' mentions all the enjoyable activities which the poet has got to do like watch web series and movies and cook and bake along with regularly calling up her folks and friends in the Pandemic.*

The Pandemic ushered in a new lifestyle

and watching web series and movies makes me smile

Be it Netflix Hotstar or Amazon Prime

All have content rich and sublime

and from them there's a lot to learn and imbibe

and to some views I fully subscribe

My 'me time ' I'm enjoying thoroughly

and it's just lovely, bonding with friends and family

I've also enjoyed baking and cooking new delicacies

and all the while making memories,

these Pandemic pleasures did bring,

the extra zest and zing,

and will continue to do so,

even after the pandemic from our lives we throw

In A Happy Space

'In A Happy Space ' is a positive poem, in which the poet expresses her happy feelings as she is at ease with herself and her environment. The poem uplifts one's mood and spirits.

I'm in a happy space and I know why

because nowadays too hard I don't try

to be in the good books of people around me

even when it comes to my dear friends and family

Although I 'd love to be as giving as I can,

from them, I wouldn't want to expect much

And when my new found thinking I scan

I discover that as I loosen myself from the clutch

of endless expectations from others, I feel lighter...

and my inner being glows brighter;

I'm in a happy space as I'm learning to let go

and the aftermath, beautifully does show.

Happiness

In the poem 'Happiness' the poet expresses her views on happiness eloquently. The poem has engaging similes and an impressive rhythm.

Happiness is elusive like a butterfly

To chase it, the more you try

the farther it will fly, leaving you, high and dry...

Look within and that's where it does lie

There's happiness in peaceful and harmonious living

There's happiness in giving

There's happiness in the smiles you bring

There's happiness when you cling

to faith, optimism and goodness

There's happiness when you overcome stress

There's happiness in all the things you painstakingly do

There's happiness when you are sincere and true

Happiness which is hedonistic, soon dies

but when divided, it multiplies

Happiness is like quicksand which can't be caught

but in your kind deeds and words, it, you can spot

The good thing is, happiness is in your hands

and this your heart understands.

My Dreams

*The poem **'My Dreams'** deals with the poet's desire to work towards fulfilling her dreams with enthusiasm and determination, come what may.*

Dreams appear in my sleep

and even when I'm awake;

sometimes they beg and weep,

beseeching me with a jerk and a shake

to make them alive

and I smilingly tell them, that I'll assiduously strive

and leave no stone unturned to make them come true

My dreams assure me that they're worth pursuing

and at times create a hullabaloo,

urging and egging me to start viewing

my life, with them, actualized....

and then I've realized,

that my dreams constantly fuel me to be,

persevering with my 'achieving spree'

and help me, to be tenacious and tough

Well truly, I can't thank my dreams enough!

Why?

*'**Why**' is a thought provoking and insightful poem wherein the poet asks relevant questions which are worth questioning and which the readers can identify with as well.*

My mind is going through a questioning wave

For others' approval why do we crave?

Why is self-acknowledgement not good enough?

Why does others' disapproval make us so glum?

and our confidence, why does it snuff?

In turn making us feel like scum?

Why do we wait for our grudges to accumulate, till we just explode?

Why do we easily resign to our fate?

Why do we rarely take the less travelled road?

Others, why do we blame so quickly?

Well! This fusillade of questions has set me free,

as I realize, I need to abandon my flawed mindset,

without getting indignant and upset

Lockdown Time

'Lockdown Time' is a simple and rhythmic poem which illustrates the need to utilize the 'Lockdown Duration ' in the best possible way.

'Lockdown Time' is so sublime

Full of peace and Tranquility; and equips us

with every facility, to make the most of it

and enjoy every bit.

There's lots to read, write, watch and creatively do

and it feels too good to be true.

Lock down time is an opportunity to reconnect and
strengthen ties

and realize that when our skills we productively utilize,

we are in for a lovely surprise.

Power Of The Pandemic

'Power of the Pandemic' talks convincingly about the positive impact which it has on her. The images and rhythm are noteworthy

Life's not the same and nor am I...

and with relief my changed self, makes me sigh

I've loved the philosophical and introspective facet

which my personality seems to lovingly embrace,

as it convinces me to efface

my agitated state when I fume and fret

And compose myself, I do, and let peace prevail

I like the way I sail smoothly over rough waves

and I assuredly silence each internal wail

and you should see how my inner self raves

about my changed disposition and temperament

Truly some golden moments with myself I've spent

I've become more confident of my abilities

Yes! a new countenance in the mirror my eyes do see

which puts me totally at ease...

as I celebrate a new me.

Feelings Of Pandemic

'Feelings of Pandemic' uses personification effectively. In this poem the Pandemic expresses its feelings regarding its arrival and the consequences that follow, as a human being. It's an interesting and unusual poem, from the point of view of the Pandemic.

I never thought that so much of turbulence I would cause,

that would shake the world and make it pause

till it switched to another mode,

where online functioning and computer code

would become the prominent highlights.

I never felt I'd be a witness to such saddening sights...

Seeing so many people die,

did make me shudder and cry

As did, people's careless and reckless streak,

that would make me question their cheek

on seeing them without masks and social distancing

my hands in despair I would wring;

Vaccines are being made to throw me out,

and exit I will, no doubt…

Not before admitting, that to mankind a lot I taught

and a lot of happiness I got

seeing people bonding and reconnecting

I wonder, me, how humans would be remembering?

About The Pandemic

*'**About the Pandemic**' talks about the lessons that the Pandemic taught and the outcome that the pandemic will have. It's got a pensive side which is compelling.*

These trying times will pass

and back to normal life will be;

but we'll cherish the 'en masse'

learning, from the pandemic and the new points of view it made us see.

Of life's unpredictability and frailty, we were reminded so blatantly,

that all we ask and pray is, may God make this earth pandemic free.

Call it Karma, Destiny or Fate,

It's been a turning point, with a spate

of changes, unforeseen and rewarding.

Yes! To the other side, the pendulum will swing,

Needless to say, a lot of happiness that will bring....

and the 'Pandemic Life Lessons' will arm us,

For a new beginning.

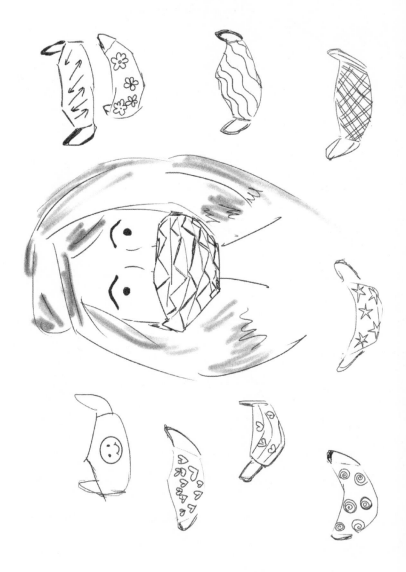

My Masks

*'**My Masks**' is a pertinent poem that describes the importance and relevance of wearing masks in these Pandemic times. The poet has infused metaphors and rhythm to make the poem appealing.*

The masks which I now use,

are not a part of a ruse,

to dissemble facets of mine,

which, with myself, I don't want to align.

They aren't garbs of pretension and sham

They aren't symbols of deceit and trickery

My masks don't mystify who I am...

On the contrary, they envelope me in a layer of safety and security

and myself as a responsible and a law-abiding citizen, I see

When my masks, without them, see me,

they seem to make a plea

to take care and have them on,

till a pandemic free day is born.

My Inner Voice

In 'My Inner Voice' the poet talks about the influence her inner voice has had on her in the pandemic and the need to connect with it and listen to it.

Prior to the Pandemic my inner voice had drowned

in a sea of voices which did abound

in cacophony, that stifled my inner dialogues

which to my mind are like cogs,

helping it to stay, composed and self-assured

But now I feel completely cured,

as my inner voice I carefully hear

ironed out are countless creases

with reasoning and cheer

and to be agitated and upset my mind ceases,

I'm ecstatic to see my inner voice emerge strong,

and very thankful to it, for befriending me all along.

Amidst The Pandemic

'Amidst the Pandemic' deals with the positive and powerful impact the Pandemic has had on the poet and has a natural flow.

I've realised, amidst the pandemic,

that life is beautiful still

Though to some guidelines I need to stick,

seeking happiness and solace is not as uphill

as it seemed to me, initially

And now my happiness, as my responsibility, I see

For happiness I no longer wait...

I've begun to consciously enjoy and appreciate

my daily chores and my changed routine

A lot more to me now, life does mean,

which has brought new perspectives in its sway,

which have made my mind as flexible as clay

and I've also realised that come what may,

Optimistic and positive I need to stay.

Mindfulness

*In the poem **'Mindfulness'** the poet demonstrates deftly how she practises it and observes its positive after effects. The anaphoric style, adds to the robustness in the poem.*

Ever since, the Pandemic on our planet has entered,

I'm practising mindfulness in the true sense of the word

I'm mindful of my thoughts, I'm mindful of my actions,

I'm mindful of my attitude, and my interactions,

I'm mindful of my eating habits and my lifestyle,

I'm mindful of my prayers, my silence and my smile,

and I'm mindful of learning new skills

and I'm mindful of the way my positivity spills

and I'm mindful of acknowledging my mindfulness

and that has largely brought down my levels of stress.

I'm mindful of being thankful to God, more than ever

and to keep up my mindfulness I'll surely endeavour!

Pondering

*'**Pondering**' effectively touches upon the quality of acceptance and looking inwards to overcome problems. It's an insightful and interesting poem.*

Who would have ever thought

that life would take such a turn?

And as I tried to discern and learn

how exactly this pandemic spread,

I was fraught with worry, shock and disbelief

and then to my relief...

I changed my lens

and mindfully practised 'acceptance'

and it worked wonders, to say the least;

It felt nice, to make my inner voice my priest

and tune inwards to duly deal,

with the consequences of the pandemic, unforeseen

and in so doing, myself I began to heal

and don't I feel sanguine and serene?

I'd love to be this changed person who I inwardly see,

even when life moves towards normalcy.

Pandemic Pursuit

In the 'Pandemic Pursuit,' the poet talks about pursuing writing poems in the times of the pandemic and expresses satisfaction when she observes the way her poems turn out.

Basking in the sun and gazing at the lawn

and letting the creative juices flow

as I put my thinking cap on

and let my inner self glow

I pen down my thoughts, feelings, ideas and views,

which with rhyme and rhythm I like to fuse,

I love the way words take on a new form and shape

at times leaving me wondrously agape

It's a stimulating and rewarding bout

and I like the way my composition pans out,

leaving me all charged up to share

my poems with those who care

to read, rate and guide

Most certainly! I'd love to have this prominent pandemic
pursuit by my side.

Valuing The Present

'Valuing the Present' is about the importance of the 'here and the now' and the need to value the present to make the most of life. The poem is simple and appealing.

Todays will turn into yesterdays,

The present will be a thing of the past;

And whichever way time sways

It's up to us to stay happy and have a blast,

And look at the sunny side,

Even when we are swimming against the tide.

Every moment of the present will be a memory,

So let's soak ourselves cheerfully,

In the 'here and now' of life

Even as we deal with each obstacle and strife,

it's up to us to try and be happy

and immerse our present in positivity

Women's Health

*'**Women's Health** ' emphasizes on the fact that women need to take care of themselves just the way they take care of their family members. The poem is relevant and conveys a powerful message.*

It is high time we Women guarded our health,

which indeed is our greatest wealth;

The nuclei of our households we form

and whenever our folks face a conflict or an internal storm,

they invariably turn to us

and patiently listen and help we do, without any fuss

We place the needs of our 'Kith & Kin' before ours always

and that's how... neglected our health stays.

Let's not continue to wait...

till it gets too late

Our Health should, in our 'Priorities list', in the top slot, fall

and we should promptly address

our health issues, big & small,

and regularly visit & follow doctors we must

for far too long our concerns have gathered dust

Now on this front let's spread awareness all around

and most importantly let's touch a new ground.

Time

*'**Time**' is an engaging and engrossing poem in which the poet presents her personal views on time in an interesting manner.*

Time waits for no one. It has its own pace.

Sometimes it crawls, sometimes it appears to race

and accordingly adjust to it and face

with courage and grace

we have to; as it shows,

along with the highs, also the lugubrious lows.

Time doesn't halt / pause / take a break

and has us all wrapped in its wake;

Time is precious, Time is powerful,

And its rhythm and flow, manages to pull

all of humanity,

which rightly honours and acknowledges its gravity,

in the best possible way,

by making the most of it each day.

Thanks To Corona

'Thanks to Corona' is a pertinent poem in which the poet thanks Corona for the positive changes that have come about in her life like being able to enjoy nature more, spending time with herself etc. It has universal appeal.

In the beauty of nature, I've begun to revel,

I've begun to dwell,

on thankfulness & gratefulness like never before;

My feelings I've begun to freely pour

and I've let my imagination soar,

and now I feel... myself, why did I ignore?

Caught up I was in the mechanical grind of my routine

and oblivious to many facets I had been

Corona has taught me

how important it is to live holistically

and a brighter canvas I see,

which fills me with delight and glee.

Ways Of The World

'Ways of the World' *portrays a realistic picture about the harsh realities of the world. It's thought provoking and profound.*

To me, as my mind, has frequently unfurled

the ways of the world,

I've accepted them with mixed feelings,

and have come to core matters after discarding peelings

'Laugh and the world laughs with you

Cry and you cry alone'

and many people I have known

who, demonstrate this view

'Success has many fathers. Failure has none'

and to take failure in one's stride,

is easier said than done,

as one's disappointment is difficult to hide.

Though genuine praises and kind words don't cost much,

and a smile on the lips of the receiver they bring,

not many are giving and generous when it comes to
complimenting

Not many have a humane touch...

Having said this... I feel in our own way

We can deviate from these ways, what say?

The Lockdown Has Taught

*'**The Lockdown Has Taught**' is another positive poem that deals with all the teaching that the Lockdown brought with it and how it benefitted us. It's got an upbeat feel and is inspiring.*

The lockdown has made us fully aware

about life's unpredictability and taught us to spare

some time to value and appreciate life's simple pleasures

And realise that connecting and bonding with people is one
of life's greatest treasures.

The lockdown has taught us new skills

and this teaching fills

our heart with confidence and a sense of achievement.

I experienced it, when for the first time, my poem, on all
poetry.com I sent.

The lockdown has taught us to stay optimistic and strong

as it stretches long

and... most importantly,

It has taught us to keep smiling and be happy.

Rhythm Of Life

In 'Rhythm of Life' the poet dexterously describes the rhythm which nature abounds in. The poem has good prosody and metre and noteworthy onomatopoeia

Life has its own rhythm in a series of quotidian occurrences

which In my mind like a reel happily whizz

The sound of the mixer whirring,

the sound of the spoon while stirring,

have a rhythm of their own

and appreciative of it I've recently grown.

There's rhythm in the ticking of the clock,

also, in the way we talk and walk;

Unmistakable is the rhythm of a chugging train

and not to forget the pitter patter of the rain

There's a definite rhythm in the chirping of birds

and in the bleating of cattle herds,

There's rhythm in the movement of a swing

and towards these sounds I'm gravitating

deeper than before...

Surely the 'rhythm of life' has me, asking for more

and my heart tells me...there's a lot in store

which corresponds to the rhythm of my life, that I'd like to explore.

Words

*The poem **'Words'** aptly describes the importance of words and the need to use words wisely. The rhythmic cadence in the poem is noteworthy and so are the images.*

Words are like arrows

which cannot be taken back, after being used

While kind words have us chirping like sparrows,

harsh words, have our mood suffused

with sadness and dismay,

and at times have us grouching and sulking all day

Had I had my way

I would keep harmful words always at bay

and would prevent others from using them too

and wonders to our relations wouldn't that do?

When used right, words are a blessing and a boon

and to enjoy them, only we humans have the fortune.

This Life

*'**This Life** ' is a contemplative and incisive poem in which the poet expresses her disturbed mental state and the need to overcome it. The poem has remarkable rhythm and meter.*

This life is all I've got...

to utilize, to enjoy and to sort

differences, conflicts and issues...all

and yet...

I get entangled in my web

of irritants and pettiness where I crawl

and their negative flow doesn't easily ebb

On the contrary, me, these mental blocks, bully

and wreak havoc; till I throw them forcefully.

This life is all I've got

to put into action every worthwhile thought,

and yet I'm caught

in my own mindless mess...for what??

This life is all I've got

to appreciate and value what I'm taught...

And as all this I express,

let me confess

My resolve is steelier than ever

to never say never.

Learning

*In **'Learning'** the poet talks about the importance and significance that learning has among human beings. The poem has an appealing pace and rhythm*

Our parents lay the foundation of learning

and coupled with our yearning

to hone and diversify our skills

we are on a roll

Our tryst with learning fills

the heart, mind and soul

with passion, determination and conviction

to turn into reality, what others perceive as fiction

Spurred we are to learn

from anyone who lets the fire in our bellies burn,

Teachers, Friends, People, Nature, Time and life itself

as long as, we don't put our desire to learn on a shelf

Learning is much needed. Learning is Fun

and it feels nice when ourselves we stun.

We As Teachers Need To

'We as Teachers Need To' delves into the quality and traits which teachers need to possess in order to ensure that students show all round development.

We teachers need to impart moral values

apart from the regular subjects at school

We need to let students freely express their views

and enable them to keep their sensibility and cool

We need to encourage them to think out of the box

We need to help them stay away from petty talks

We need to patiently listen to them to make our
communication progress

We need to teach them to stay away from peer pressure and
stress

We need to go way beyond academics and help them be

Citizens conscientious and trust worthy

Beauty

*'**Beauty**' is a unique kind of a poem in which the poet brings in, her own perspective about 'Beauty wherein she expresses adeptly the expanse of beauty which goes beyond the physical form.*

The expanse of beauty is immense

and it goes beyond external physical appearance

The beauty of goodness and the human spirit,

and of courage of conviction and grit,

together with a magnanimous heart

has gravitas that stands apart.

The beauty of one's conscience and soul

and one's self - control,

has an aura ever so mesmerizing

There's beauty in our way of realizing and visualizing.

Ah! There's beauty in many a thing, hence,

we need to be receptive to its extensive presence.

Change

*'**Change'** is an engrossing poem which describes change dexterously. The impressive rhythm and pace are worth mentioning too.*

The only constant in life is change

and that does sound strange

but it's a way of life

and though it causes conflict and strife

Our very evolution on it, thrives,

and it adds to the momentum and purpose of our lives.

Our thoughts, our perspectives and priorities

change with time, as do our memories

Be it our choices in food, fashion and friends

Choosing never ends.

There are some changes that happen to us,

Over which we kick up a row and fuss

but over them we have no control

and they turn out to be 'life altering' experiences and uplift
the soul.

Change is inescapable, Change is imperative

and with it I'm learning to happily live.

Life Is

*'**Life Is**' is a rich and symbolic poem in which the poet looks at life in a philosophical yet convincing manner.*

Life is, how we perceive what we see

from the prism of our perceptions and point of view

and how we react to them and choose to be.

Life is, mastering skills myriad and new

and vibrating with vivacity and vibrancy

and soaking up each enriching shade and hue

and submerging ourselves totally

in the here and now and giving ourselves the due

as the minutes of magical moments we enjoy

and learn to leave out things that annoy.

Life is, letting our inner voice listen to our plea

of loving ourselves wholeheartedly

Life is, being comfortable in our own skin

Life is, letting our spirit and morale win.

My Persona

*'**My Persona**' is a reflective and rhythmic poem which skillfully limns the way poet perceives her persona and about the factors which influence it.*

My persona, mirrors my inner struggles

and myriad moods, which my mind juggles.

It reflects a plethora of emotions

and my reaction to ideas and notions

and a welter of situations and experiences

which fill up my senses,

in a miscellaneous way

and yet I try to keep at bay

dismay, dejection and despair,

even as I accept, that my persona will bear

these unflattering giveaways...

I hope the longing to be and look happy stays.

My Greys

*'**My Greys**' is a candid poem in which the poet acknowledges the dignity and sobriety which her grey hair brings to her personality and honours their contribution.*

I find the greys on my head intriguing

and admire the dignity and character they bring

to my personality and bearing

Earlier their appearance would sting

my self-image and I would feel so so low

and off to the parlour to dye them I would go

But now I've learned

that every grey streak that I've earned

tells a story of experience and maturity

And no... far from indulging in self pity

to my appearance they lend an air of sobriety

These days I let my greys stay a little longer

and colour them when the need to camouflage gets
stronger...

and out of shame them I no longer want to shoo

as I respect and honour them, through and through.

Making Memories

*'**Making Memories**' very gently stresses on the importance of having pleasant memories in our lives as they refresh us from time to time and keep us in good spirits.*

When I smile ever so lovingly,

and unrestrainedly laugh, when I warmly hug,

when I speak sweetly, and give with glee,

I'm creating memories, so cozy and snug

and their comforting companionship as I often seek,

My 'joie de vivre' touches a new peak...

When I go out of my way to help and support

My spirits in the sky float

and these memories I'd like to freeze

as they never cease to soothe and please

Some memories happen and many have to be made

wherein, ourselves we have to rightly aid

I Choose

'I Choose' is a personal poem in which the poet focuses on her priorities and preferences. The rhythm and anaphoric style add to the appeal.

I choose to see ways to bloom

I choose to refuse despondency and gloom

I choose to smile and laugh

and improve my 'mood graph'

I choose to see the brighter side

I choose to be my own friend and guide

I choose to be optimistic to the core

as I feel there's lots to learn and explore...

I choose to be stoic and strong

as I've wallowed in self-pity and misery too long

I choose to start afresh...anew,

Appreciating the way my life I view

We Rise

'We Rise' is a philosophical poem which highlights the importance of good conduct and deeds and its positive impact on us.

When we help others and help them rise,

Rise in our own eyes we do;

And we realise that our happiness lies,

in seeing and making others happy too.

We rise above ourselves when to others we reach out

despite our inhibitions and nagging self-doubt;

We rise when we smile and politely talk,

and in so doing ourselves we pleasantly shock,

while venom we want to spew

and we rise when we bid adieu

to bickering and nitpicking.

Well! I'm rising...and it's exciting!

Challenging Days

'Challenging Days' depicts the need to make the most of each day however difficult and challenging it may be. The rhythm and images in the poem make it fascinating.

There will be all kinds of days

Some energizing like the sun's rays,

some languid, in which we'd want to loll & laze,

some will bring in a new fad, a new craze,

some will be a haze

where life will be a maze,

some will have us in a daze

But our challenge is to (try to) be happy always,

to accept life's unchangeable ways

yet follow what our heart says,

and resolutely chase

our dreams with our enthusiasm ablaze.

Realization

'Realization' talks impressively about the poet's expression and how it delightfully surprises her. The poem is trenchant and riveting.

Ever since I've begun to pay special attention

towards my expression, oral and written,

I have to mention

that I'm completely smitten

by the richness and rhythm that words unfold,

and many a time what is created is pure gold;

My expression reflects influences umpteen,

and to analyse them, watchful as a hawk I've been.

As I track the way my words flow,

I'm pleased with the maturity they show

My expression has helped me grow

more sensitive and empathetic

More importantly it has helped me to rightly know,

that I have to like it first to make it click

and when my doubts, my self-approval will throw,

a long way indeed I will go.

Cogitation

*'**Cogitation**' presents the poet's philosophical views in a striking manner. The poet is intense and insightful.*

Everybody's personal journey is distinct and unique

and we all have our own battles to fight

We have our own answers to seek

and our own perceptions of wrong and right

We have our own problems and difficulties to deal

and a grim side that we like to conceal

We all have our share of sorrow failures and pain

So next time I'll consciously refrain

from passing judgment even in my head

I'll try and be more empathetic instead

and from constant comparisons I'll stay far away

Oh dear! The Pandemic has matured me, I must say...

Words of Caution

In this poem the poet shares her invaluable life lessons. The poem is profound philosophical and impactful.

Words of Caution

When you don't want to talk, remain silent

Compose yourself, to prevent getting het up and violent

Lock your mouth when you are about to blurt,

something...that'll sadden and hurt,

the hearer, because to your impulses, you give in

At others failures, don't laugh and grin,

Don't be afraid to gently say things, as you feel...

Well! With the consequences, you will learn to deal,

Say 'No' when you need to

and decide, whose words, are worth paying, heed to

Don't open your heart to many,

as your personal secrets will reach countless ears, without

costing any, a penny

and the distorted versions, will land you in tears....

Your pent-up feelings, try to thoughtfully release

and others, don't try too hard to please...

I've learnt these lessons the hard way

But...may your road be smoother...I pray

Made in the USA
Las Vegas, NV
20 September 2021